THE BABY ANIMAL ABC

Drawn by
Robert Broomfield

PUFFIN BOOKS
in association with The Bodley Head

G000140288

a

anteater cub

A

ANTEATER

B
BISON

b
bison calf

C
COW

C
calf

D

DONKEY

d

donkey
foal

E

ELEPHANT

e

elephant calf

F
FOX

f
fox cubs

G

GOAT

g

goat kid

H

HEDGEHOG

h

hedgehog
young

I

IMPALA

i

impala
fawn

J

JAGUAR

j jaguar cubs

k

koala cub

K

KOALA

L

LION

1

lion cubs

M

MONKEY

m

monkey
baby

N

NEWT

n

**newt
young**

O

OWL

owlets

P

PONY

p

pony foal

Q

QUAIL

q

quail chicks

R

RHINOCEROS

r

rhinoceros
calf

S

SEAL

S

seal
pup

T

TIGER

t

tiger
cubs

U

URIAL

u

urial lamb

V
VOLE

v
vole babies

W WOLF

w wolf cubs

X

XERUS

X

xerus young

Y

YAK

y

yak calf

Z

ZEBRA

z

zebra
foal